# STANLEY

# GOD
## IS IN CONTROL

AN UNSHAKABLE PEACE IN THE MIDST OF LIFE'S STORMS

COUNTRYMAN
®

NASHVILLE, TENNESSEE

Editor: Pat Matuszak

Project Editor: Kathy Baker

Design: Lookout Design Group, Inc., Minneapolis, Minnesota

ISBN 0-8499-5739-7

Printed and bound in Belgium

www.thomasnelson.com
www.jcountryman.com
www.intouch.org

GOD

IS IN EVERYTHING

# Never forget, God Is in Control.

I recall that in one of the most painful and difficult seasons of my life—a time when I felt very discouraged and fearful—when moments of loneliness were most intense, I would seek out my best friend for his wisdom. Often he and I would sit by the fire for hours in the evening and talk. He would encourage me to pour out my heart about how I was feeling—all about the incredible pain that seemed to flood my soul. Over and over again he would say to me, "Remember, Charles, God is in control." That factual statement became an anchor to my life. No matter how hard the wind began to blow or how much the adversity seemed to intensify, my soul remained anchored to that simple truth: God really is in control.

## STRENGTH AND POWER...

When a person can come to the place in life where they can say with absolute unwavering conviction, "Yes, but my God is in control," there is an awesome sense of strength and assurance that will fill the heart to overflow with an indescribable joy and peace. No matter what the challenges we face in life, this peace can remain.

# Is God in everything?

It's a tough question, but one that every Christian must clearly answer.

### IS GOD IN EVERYTHING?

My answer to this question reflects my confidence in Him. It directly impacts my reaction in the midst of life's storms.

### IS GOD IN EVERYTHING?

It makes the difference as to whether I will be able to experience contentment in the time of trial. My answer directly determines how obedient I will be to His will for my life.

Is God in everything in your life?
Paul teaches, "in everything give thanks . . . "
(1 Thessalonians 5:18). If God is not in everything, can I
honestly give thanks for everything?

Assurance and Confidence...
Paul clarifies this idea of giving thanks when he writes:

> And we know that God causes all things to work
>
> together for good to those who love God,
>
> to those who are called according to His purpose
>
> For those whom He foreknew, He also predestined
>
> to become conformed to the image of His Son,
>
> that He would be the firstborn among many
>
> brethren. —Romans 8:28-29 NASB

## Remember this...

The Bible says, "The angel of the LORD encamps all around those who fear Him, and delivers them" (Psalm 34:7). So, every single one of His children is encircled by the presence of almighty God!

This means that literally every test or trial—whether it is in our jobs, finances, families, or health, whatever it may be— has to happen in the presence of our loving heavenly Father. He has allowed it. That's the only way. He is in everything.

## Sometimes we suffer...

because of other people's failures, their sins or their ignorance.
We can respond in one of two ways:

We can be resentful, hostile and angry. We can place blame
and seek vengeance.

Or, we can say, "God, You are working everything together
for good. You didn't say I would like it. You didn't promise it
would be pleasant. What do You want to teach me in this
circumstance?"

# None of us like to suffer...

and we have a right to say, "God, I don't like it. I don't understand why." We can argue with Him, tell Him exactly how we feel. Just let Him know, "Father, I don't like anything about this. I feel it's unfair, it's unjust." Go ahead and tell Him. Open up your heart. He fully understands.

## It's okay to cry.

It's natural to weep. Tell God: "I'm weak. I failed." Confess
to Him, "I've sinned." He understands when you say, "God,
I just can't handle some things."

Never think, "Christians don't cry." Remember,
Jesus cried.

Never say, "Christians can't show weakness." Paul said,
"When I feel as if the bottom has dropped out and I don't
feel one ounce of energy, strength, or resistance within me,
then I experience the mighty grace of my almighty God."
(2 Corinthians 12:9, paraphrase)

## God is in everything:

even the things in life that we do not like,
even the things in life that cause us pain.

Because you're a child of God, He holds every circumstance
in His hand.

You see, the heart of man is in the hand of God,
and like the waters He turns it whithersoever He will.
(Proverbs 21:1, paraphrase)

# God cares for you

Remember these assurances?

> Our Lord says He watches the sparrow that falls, and every
> hair upon our head is numbered. (Matthew 10:29-30)
> He clothes the lilies of the field. (Matthew 6:28-29)

God says,

> **"For My thoughts are not your thoughts,**
>
> **Nor are your ways My ways, says the Lord.**
>
> **For as the heavens are higher than the earth,**
>
> **So are My ways higher than your ways,**
>
> **And My thoughts than your thoughts."** —Isaiah 55:8-9

Here is a Scripure that you should mark in your Bible.
Underline it and the next time you face something that
you absolutely cannot understand, remember this:

> **"The secret things belong to the Lord our God,**
>
> **but the things revealed belong to us and to**
>
> **our children forever, that we may follow all**
>
> **the words of this law"** —Deuteronomy 29:29 NASB

There are some questions for which I will never have a satisfactory answer.

Not that satisfies in this life.

There are some things I don't understand, and there are some things I may be able to logically reason out. But, ultimately, there are some things that God is going to keep a secret until we get to heaven.


Open the Word and see what God says.

When we come to those challenges—
difficult times that strike us where we hurt,
and we don't quite understand—

let's first of all establish in our heart the eternal truth . . .
God is in control.

In just a few verses of Psalm 103, David expresses a truth that
he held close to his heart. More than likely, he learned this
truth the way most of us have to learn it—by personal
experience.

Today, we are blessed . . .

> The LORD has established His throne in
>
> the heavens; and His sovereignty rules over all.
>
> Bless the LORD, you His angels, mighty in
>
> strength, who perform His word, obeying
>
> the voice of His word!
>
> Bless the LORD, all you His hosts, you who
>
> serve Him, doing His will.
>
> Bless the LORD, all you works of His, in
>
> all places of His dominion; bless the LORD,
>
> O my soul! —Psalm 103:19-22 NASB

# Alpha and Omega

From Genesis to Revelation, here's the central message:
God Almighty, the Lord Jesus Christ, the Spirit of God,
the Triune God is in control of all things, period. God uses
life to prove it, starting in the first chapter of the Bible
with verse one:

> **In the beginning God created the heavens
> and the earth.** —Genesis 1:1

Listen,
Almighty God created this world out of nothing,
put it into space,
created all the galaxies in the universe,
put the laws of nature in motion,
and governs and guides His creation.

Certainly, He is in control of it.

Not only did He create the universe, but He sustains it and
keeps it. That's exactly what Paul describes in Colossians,
chapter 1.

God's sovereignty is beautifully expressed in this passage:

He is the image of the invisible God, the firstborn over all creation. For by Him all things were created that are in heaven and that are on earth, visible and invisible, whether thrones or dominions or principalities or powers. All things were created through Him and for Him. And He is before all things, and in Him all things consist. And He is the head of the body, the church, who is the beginning, the firstborn from the dead, that in all things He may have the preeminence. For it pleased the Father that in Him all the fullness should dwell, and by Him to reconcile all things to Himself, by Him, whether things on earth or things in heaven, having made peace through the blood of His cross. —Colossians 1:15-20

# God's not in the business of chance.

God is in the blessing business.

There's no such thing as chance with Him. Yes, God provides opportunities in life, but He does not make things lucky for people.

You may feel that you are unlucky or that your life is out of control. You may not believe areas in your life are the way they ought to be. But God has not lost control of your life. You might have been trying to control it yourself, and circumstances might have gone astray because you've gotten out of God's will. Or it may be that God has allowed hardship in your life because He is preparing for what He knows will turn out for good.

Just because we do not understand all the ways of God does not mean that He is out of control of my life!

Does God have a plan? Absolutely! Does He do anything without a specific reason and a design? No, He does not.

You see, God would not bring you into this world and just say, "Do the best you can."

# He is Lord

You and I could read through the entire Bible—from Genesis to Revelation—and here's what we would find:

Jesus Christ is the sovereign Lord of this earth.

As John unfolds the Revelation, we see that He is:
> Lord in the Revelation,
> Lord during the times of the Great Tribulation,
> Lord in His Second Coming.
> Lord in the Judgment,
> Lord in Heaven.

God is in absolute control, and the Bible is simply a beautiful expression of how He demonstrates love for mankind. The Word is filled with wonderful promises He is willing to do in the lives of those who submit to Him.

You'll not find God's servants in the Scripture talking about things just happening.

See it for yourself. Listen to what the psalmist says:

> **For I know that the LORD is great, and our LORD is above all gods. Whatever the LORD pleases, He does . . .** —Psalm 135:5-6

Now, did you get that? Whatever the Lord pleases, He does. A lot of people would like to be able to do that, wouldn't they? But in reality the only being who can do that with supreme and total understanding is almighty God. He alone has the ability to understand life from its beginning to its end. He finds ultimate pleasure in helping us fulfill His plan for our lives.

Whatever pleases God, He does.

He did not promise, "And you will always understand My actions."

There will be times when I won't understand what He does. But God's in charge. Listen,

> Whatever the LORD pleases, He does, in heaven
> and in earth, in the seas and in all deep places.
> He causes the vapors to ascend from the ends
> of the earth; He makes lightning for the rain;
> He brings the wind out of His treasuries.
>
> —Psalm 135:6-7

Now, let's look at Joseph as an example of not understanding life's circumstances. His brothers tried to kill him, sold him as a slave and tried to forget him, and then they came back to him for help. But God lifted Joseph out of trouble and he became, at the age of thirty, the prime minister of Egypt and saved the whole nation from famine. Look what Joseph says to his estranged brothers:

> Joseph said to them, "Do not be afraid, for am
> I in God's place? As for you, you meant evil
> against me, but God meant it for good in
> order to bring about this present result, to
> preserve many people alive. —Genesis 50:19-20 NASB

What motivated Joseph's enemies? Ill will, anger, bitterness, resentment, hostility, and jealousy. Why would God allow such evil people to do such wicked things to a young man who was so obedient to the Father? That doesn't seem fair.

During all those years of suffering, trial, and heartache—being imprisoned, framed for attempted rape, and forgotten—it looked as if God had forgotten Joseph. But if Joseph's attitude had been, "One of these days I'm going to get even," events would have turned out differently for him. When he became the prime minister, if his attitude had been, "Now it's time for vengeance," and the first time he had seen his brothers, if he had said, "Well, well, well, am I going to fix you. You thought you got rid of me. You just wait," God would never have allowed him to become the prime minister of Egypt.

You see, Joseph was wise enough that no matter what the circumstances, he saw it as coming from God's hand. As Joseph said, "You meant it for evil. God meant it for good."

Think about this. How else would God have taken this Hebrew and moved him down to Egypt, taught him Egyptian culture and language and made him the prime minister of all of Egypt? God used Joseph's brothers' wicked acts. Although he did not know why all this was happening, Joseph's response was, "God, You're still God. You are in everything. You are in all this."

You know how God responded? He made him the prime minister.

## God can use adversity.

Do you know why we sometimes stay in trouble and things don't work out? We cry out to God, but then we look at our circumstances, we find other people to blame, we become resentful, hostile, angry—it's a vicious cycle. We wonder, "Father, where in the world are You? God, if You love me, why do these things happen?"

But when we finally discern, "This situation is from God's hand," do you know what is going to happen? The adversity will either change or disappear.

Friend, God is in everything, even the things in life that you do not like, things in life that cause you pain and sorrow.

There will be times when you want to run a thousand miles in the other direction and say, "God, I can't handle any more of this."

So God says, "Then you don't want to change."

You say, "But God, that's not from You. That's from him. It's from her. It's from them." No. You see, because you're a child of God, His hand, ultimately, holds every trial. He can use every adversity.

Is God in everything? According to what the Word says, "God causes all things to work together for good . . ." (Romans 8:28, NASB). Just in time God demonstrates His awesome, irresistible power.

What can you do about an earthquake? You can't stop it. What about a volcanic eruption? You can't change its course. What about a hurricane? You can't quiet its rage. What about a tornado? You can't stop it.

Yes, God's in everything. In one way or another, God is in everything.

What about the unbeliever? Is God in everything for that person? Yes and no. He is in everything that happens in the life of the unbeliever in this light:

God knows everything the unbeliever does.
He is continually extending His love to the unbeliever.
He is continually reaching out, ready and willing to forgive.
He is continually attempting to convict the unbeliever of sin.

He is continually attempting to demonstrate His love so that the person will understand he or she needs Christ.

He is continually involved in the unbeliever's life. Mindful of each sin, God sees to it that there are consequences to disobedience.

That's what the Bible teaches in Ephesians chapter 5:

**Because of these things the wrath of God comes upon the sons of disobedience.** —Ephesians 5:6

Is God involved in the life
of the unbeliever?

Yes, He is.

# THE LORD

## IS MY SHEPHERD

# CHAPTER TWO

# Why would God permit tragedy?

Why would He allow a planeload of people to crash?
Is God in that? God is in everything. But why would
God allow such a horrible thing?

Well, let me ask you this. Those on the plane who
die in faith as believers, aren't they instantly in the
presence of God? Absolutely. From our viewpoint
it's a horrible disaster. But from their viewpoint
they're in glory.

Then what about the others who don't know the Lord?

Do you imagine that they just haphazardly chose to
get on that flight, that God didn't know who was
going to be on board? God knew the name of every
saint and every sinner. He knew every detail about
the lives of every single person. God's in everything.

## Revealing our hearts.

Why does God allow tragedy resulting from the acts of unbelievers to affect the lives of His children?

I believe this is the reason: God desires to reveal the wickedness, depravity and evil of men's hearts.
He uses this to shock us into a clear perspective about sin.
A society drifts—and then what happens? In cities all across America and all across the world, it is those awful things that happen to innocent people that shock us into reality.
"Something has to change," we say.

You see, if God only allowed the evil to destroy the evil, what would we say? "They got what they deserve." Then we could go on in our carefree way.

It is when the godly and the innocent suffer that we cry out, "Something must be done."

## 'The Lord is my shepherd, I shall not want...'

Psalm 23 is one of the most familiar passages in all the Bible.
I can remember when I was a schoolboy that everybody had
to memorize this Scripture. You will hear it read at almost
every single funeral. Often it is quoted at the bedside of
someone who is very ill. Many of us have read the stories of
men in battle who, in the midst of great fear, pulled out their
pocket-sized New Testament and Psalms to read:

The LORD is my shepherd, I shall not want.

    He makes me to lie down in green pastures;

    He leads me beside the still waters.

    He restores my soul;

    He leads me in the paths of righteousness

    For His name's sake.

> Yea, though I walk through the valley
>
> of the shadow of death,
>
> I will fear no evil; for You are with me;
>
> Your rod and Your staff, they comfort me.
>
> —Psalm 23:1-4

Valleys in the Bible often are indications or symbols of times of difficulty, hardship, trial, suffering, and pain. Those valley experiences are inevitable in the life of every believer, because if you have mountains, you're going to have valleys. Although most of us would like for the Christian life to be one of leaping from peak to peak.

God does not intend for us to live in the valleys as our normal way of life, but there will be those seasons in life—times of difficulty, hardship, trial, pain, rejection—that become valley experiences. They will be there.

What the psalmist is saying in this passage is, "Even though I walk through these dark valleys, I will fear no evil."

# Psalm 23 is talking about hardship and pain.

We go through suffering and trials in life. Oftentimes we feel hopeless; oftentimes we feel helpless. And no matter what anybody does for us, we feel absolutely, totally dependent upon God.

We truly are dependent upon Him. If the sheep stray away from the shepherd, they usually will end up in dangerous places.

But our Good Shepherd says He's going to take us to green pastures, quiet waters; He assures us He will restore our souls and guide us in the paths of righteousness.

## 'You are with me'

is the heart and the core of Psalm 23. It is a Psalm of comfort
and assurance, reminding us that we're going to have those
experiences of life that are so difficult and painful and hard
that the only thing we have is God.

No matter what experience you're going through, first ask
the question, "God, why am I in this valley?"

And second, "Lord, what is Your goal for me in this trial?
How should I respond to this valley experience?"

# When you weep in the valleys,

you don't just cry with your eyes—you weep from deep, down inside your spirit. In some of your walks in the valley there is indescribable pain. Everything on the inside gets tested. There seems to be some kind of reaction in your innermost being, the deepest part of your spirit.

Only a person who has been through a deep, dark, painful valley understands such pain.

Jesus said,

> "I am the good shepherd; I know my sheep and my sheep know me." —John 10:14 NIV

He also said:

> "My sheep hear My voice, and I know them, and
> they follow Me. And I give them eternal life,
> and they shall never perish; neither shall
> anyone snatch them out of my hand. My Father,
> who has given them to Me, is greater than all;
> and no one is able to snatch them out of
> My Father's hand. I and My Father are one."
>
> —John 10:27–30

This much I know: in the valley, no matter how treacherous and painful and difficult, nobody can take your hand out of the hand of the Good Shepherd.

Because you see, in the valley, you and I are not holding onto Him for dear life. It's the Good Shepherd who has taken *us* by the hand! It doesn't make any difference if we let go.

Thank God, He will never let go.

I don't know where you may be in the valley, but I can
tell you this, my friend:

## The wisest thing you can do is immerse yourself in the Bible.

Read it, pray over it, listen to the messages of God's servants—
as long as they are focused on the Word—write down the
truth, apply it to your heart, look at how it's being applied in
other people's lives, and consider the consequences of
disobedience.

Scriptural truths establish you so that, when you get into the
valley, the Lord Jesus Christ, who holds your hand every step
of the way, will keep reminding you of them. Remember what
He says? He sent the Holy Spirit in order that He may bring
to our remembrance those eternal truths (John 14:26). He does
that so you and I can apply to our heart those basic principles
that anchor us and steady us and keep us firm and solid and
stable in the most difficult, trying times of life.

In the valley, we discover the character of God
in a way that we never will on the mountain peak.

You and I will discover aspects of God in the deepest, darkest,
most treacherous valley experiences that we never could even
glimpse on the mountaintop. That's just the way life is. God
reveals Himself in the valley in a way that He does not reveal
on the mountain peak.

In valley experiences, we discover an intimacy and a
sense of quietness.

He says that He will lead us into places of rest. Listen to
me carefully: In the deepest, darkest, blackest moment of
your valley experience, there can be the most overwhelming,
indescribable sense of peace and rest—a quietness and
confidence that you could experience only when hand-in-hand
with the Son of God.

**You prepare a table before me in the
presence of my enemies . . .** —Psalm 23:5

God will provide for our needs in the darkest, deepest, most
painful part of the valley experience.

**. . . You anoint my head with oil;
My cup runs over."** —Psalm 23:5

The shepherd would take oil and rub it on those skinned
places where the sheep injured themselves. And the psalmist
is simply saying that God is going to be our Comforter; He's
going to be our Healer. When we are in the valley, once you
and I begin to respond correctly, the healing process begins
even in the most intense pain.

God doesn't wait until we're back on the mountain peak to start the healing process. That's not the way God operates. He anoints us with oil; our cup runs over. He provides everything that we need exactly when we need it.

> **Surely goodness and lovingkindness will follow me all the days of my life, And I will dwell in the house of the LORD forever.** —Psalm 23:6 NASB

When everything is going your way, it is very easy to sit in church and say, "I believe in God. Yes indeed, I do. 'Blessed assurance, Jesus is mine.' Hallelujah! Amazing grace! I believe all those songs. I believe the Bible from cover to cover."

Now let me ask you this: When the pain hits and the hopelessness is overwhelming, then what do you believe?

You see, we discover things about ourselves in the deepest, darkest valley experiences. We discover how much real courage we have. We discover the degree of our faith. We discover the focus of our faith. We discover if our self-image is based in Him, or in somebody else, or in what other people think. We discover the true nature of our character.

We discover what character is really all about when we go through those things that cause us to be absolutely helpless . . .

and all we can do is depend upon God. We discover things about ourselves. We discover what our real value system in life is all about. We discover what are our real priorities in life.

God knows how to wrench from us everything we depend upon. That's really what He's up to in the valley experience. His ultimate purpose is to remove from us—emotionally, physically or materially—every single, solitary thing so that Jesus Christ has no competition as Lord in our life. Then there are no challenges to His rule, His reign, and His lordship in our life.

If you have never trusted Jesus Christ as your personal Savior, you aren't resting in the green pastures of Psalm 23.

Until you call Him "Lord," you cannot say, "The Lord is my shepherd." You cannot say, "I shall not want." Nor can you talk about green pastures and still waters and guided paths. Those blessings come when you have asked the Lord Jesus Christ to forgive you of your sins, when you have asked Him to take you and save you by His grace through the shed blood of His Son at Calvary. The moment you confess your sins to Him and receive Him as your Savior, He not only becomes your Savior, but He becomes your Good Shepherd.

That is my prayer for you.

*Father, I am so grateful for Psalm 23.*

*This passage of Scripture is so simple, but so descriptive,*

*so comforting and so reassuring. I ask You, Father, with*

*all of my heart for all the hurting people who are reading*

*this book today and all the hurting people who are going*

*to see this, that the Spirit of God would write, etch*

*indelibly upon their heart that when You said You would*

*be with us, You meant every step of the way.*

*That You will work good out of all of the pain,*

*the hurt, and the suffering, and that You will accomplish*

*Your purpose, Your way, and Your will.*

*Father, we want to rest in that today,*

*and we thank You that You're the all-sufficient Savior,*

*adequate for every experience we face in life.*

*We thank You for it in Jesus' name. Amen.*

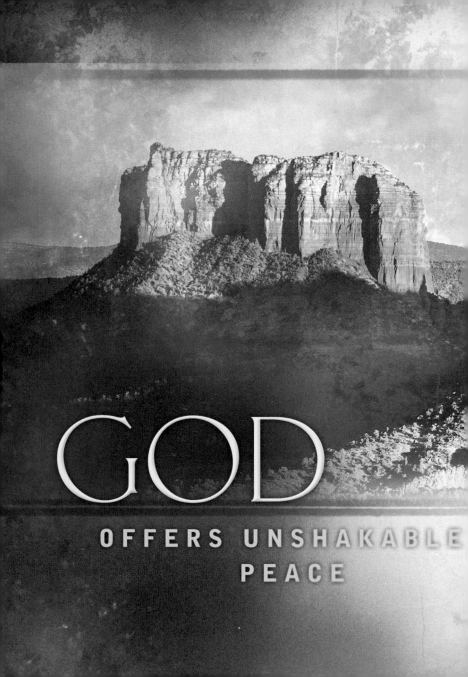

# GOD

OFFERS UNSHAKABLE
PEACE

# CHAPTER THREE

# Is it possible to have an unshakable peace?

We live in a world with so many causes for anxiety all about us, but the answer is yes. And the key to experiencing that unshakable peace is found in this passage:

**Let your gentle spirit be known to all men. The Lord is near. Be anxious for nothing, but in everything by prayer and supplication with thanksgiving let your requests be made known to God. And the peace of God, which surpasses all comprehension, will guard your hearts and minds in Christ Jesus.** —Philippians 4:5-7 NASB

## Two kinds of peace

When we think about peace, we usually think about feeling calm, but in the Scriptures there are two kinds of peace. One of them is the peace *with* God; the other is the peace *of* God.

Peace *with* God means you and I receive the Lord Jesus Christ as our personal Savior, and that decision ends the opposition between God and ourselves. He forgives us of our sins and saves us. He places us into His family. The war is over and we have become His children, no longer His enemies.

But after you and I become children of God, we still have to live in this world full of anxieties and fears and frustrations. The Bible talks about the peace *of* God that surpasses all human understanding. This peace that God gives is a peace that is not determined by circumstances.

The peace of God isn't something that you and I are brought into through some change of circumstance. Neither is it a matter of chance or of luck. It is a matter of choice.

The peace of God dwelling and ruling in our heart and mind in an unshakable fashion is a choice we make. Unshakable peace means that it is steady and strong. It is unflinching and unwavering. No matter what happens, that peace remains and we are confident and steadfast. We are not thrown off balance no matter what we face in life.

# Be anxious about nothing

What are the real causes of anxiety? A major source is inadequacy. When we don't know how to handle something, we become anxious, we become fearful, we become insecure. So we ask, "How do I deal with this?"

A second cause for anxiety is pride. We are too proud to go to God and say, "Lord, I just can't handle this. God, I don't know what to do. I am absolutely and totally dependent upon You." Or we are too proud to share our burden, our heartache, our trouble, our trial with someone else.

Let's just relax. Nobody alive has it all together. We can't solve every problem, and we can't fix everybody. People are eaten up on the inside with all kinds of anxieties and frustrations and fears because of the whole idea that we can handle it alone. That is not God's way of doing it.

# We have to be humble . . .

and admit that we are inadequate. Let's just face it. God made
each of us with needs. Now if He made me that way, why do
I want to strut around like I am in control? The truth is we
weren't made to be self-sufficient. We are not adequate.
We cannot handle things in life alone because God did not
equip us to handle life apart from Himself!

We have concerns. They are natural concerns that God
intends for us to have because He wants us to be responsible,
not irresponsible. That's what the Sermon on Mount is
talking about in the sixth chapter of Matthew: "Don't be
anxious about food, don't be anxious about clothing. Look at
the lilies of the field, the birds of the air . . . " (verses 26-34)

So, it doesn't mean "don't be responsible" but rather "don't
be anxious."

It is not God's will for us to be anxious.

The reason Paul says, "Don't be anxious about anything," is simply because we don't have to be.

We don't have to accept that "life is just that way" when we have an omnipotent God living on the inside of us. What we have to do is ask, "Lord, how do You want me to respond to this situation or this circumstance?"

# You will never be able to fix your life.

You're not going to be able to corral everything, put it together, and keep it exactly the way you want it. We just have to face the issues, difficulties, trials, and heartaches that would cause us anxieties and fears and insecurities. And so, the question is: How do we deal with them?

Remember this . . . it is the will of God for us to experience unshakable peace. Steady, steadfast, strong, unfaltering, unwavering and unflinching peace—this is how God wants us to live.

## Focus on Prayer

Paul teaches that when we feel anxious, we should consider it as a motivation to pray.

The Bible commands us to pray "for kings and all who are in authority . . ." It teaches us to pray with this in mind, " . . . so that we may lead a tranquil and quiet life in all godliness and dignity" (1 Timothy 2:2 NASB).

This means it's the will of God for communities, cities, states, and nations, that the affairs of this world be carried on in such a way—and the leaders would be so godly—that the end

result would be that people could live a tranquil and quiet
life in all godliness and dignity.

One particular night in the life of the apostles certainly
must have been the most anxious time of their lives.

We read in the gospel of John how Jesus had been showing
His disciples that He was the promised Savior, Israel's
long–awaited Messiah. Then one night as they were observing
the Passover celebration, He began speaking to them about
dying. Jesus told them He was going to leave and that one
of His trusted followers was going to betray Him.

They began asking, "Who is it Lord? Am I the one?"
They were filled with fear, disappointment, and anxiety.

But Jesus understood their feelings. Listen to His promise
to them:

"Peace I leave with you; My peace I give to you;
not as the world gives do I give to you.
Let not your heart be troubled, neither
let it be afraid." —John 14:27

In the midst of anxiety, fear, and real frustration. Jesus says, "I want to give you My peace." He says, "Don't let your heart be troubled. You don't have to be anxious in these moments. You don't have to be fearful. I want to give you a peace that will sustain you through this."

It is the will of God that you and I enjoy an unshakable peace.

God has given us the great blessing of having the Bible, God's inspired Word. It provides us the written example of how Jesus lived and what He taught. This is the living Word from our almighty God.

The Holy Spirit who indwells Christians produces His fruit in our lives. An unshakable peace is a result of His presence.

**The fruit of the Spirit is love, joy, peace, longsuffering, kindness, goodness, faithfulness, gentleness, self-control. Against such there is no law.** —Galatians 5:22-23

Paul teaches:

> **Let the peace of Christ rule in your hearts,**
>
> **to which indeed you were called in one body;**
>
> **and be thankful. Let the word of Christ richly**
>
> **dwell within you, with all wisdom teaching**
>
> **and admonishing one another with psalms**
>
> **and hymns and spiritual songs, singing with**
>
> **thankfulness in your hearts . . .**
>
> —Colossians 3:15-16 NASB

Paul encourages believers to allow the peace of God to rule in our hearts. In the midst of adversity, when we are surrounded by doubts and fears, we are to let peace settle our hearts.

You might ask, "Why?" The answer is clear—God's peace can calm any of life's storms.

# The Lord of Peace

**Now may the Lord of peace Himself continually grant you peace in every circumstance...**

—2 Thessalonians 3:16 NASB

Three simple words are the keys to understanding this Scripture: "in every circumstance." That is when God will provide His peace. Every circumstance, all circumstances, this is the key to Paul's teaching, "Do not be anxious about anything" (Philippians 4:6).

Peace is a gift. Paul reflects, may God "grant you peace." Peace isn't something I manipulate. Peace isn't something I have as a result of my own actions, my own merit. Paul says, "Now may the Lord of peace Himself give you peace."

# He is our peace

Unshakable peace is the peace of God. We find its origin in Him. If you are reborn in Him, sealed by the Holy Spirit, then you have the Source of peace. It's beyond your own understanding. Don't try to figure it out.

Paul teaches, " . . . the peace of God, which surpasses all comprehension, will guard your hearts and your minds in Christ Jesus" (Philippians 4:7 NASB). True peace protects. It will guard the way we think and safeguard our feelings.

The Greek word here for "guard" is a military term used for the sentries who guarded the palace. The quality of peace Paul refers to is the kind that "garrisons about" like a king's palace guard. God's peace cushions everything that comes our way. That's why the Bible commands, "Let it rule in your heart. Let it reign in your heart."

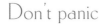

## Don't panic

When you and I learn to allow the peace of God to rule our hearts, it cushions everything that comes our way. Therefore, anxiety doesn't throw us off balance, it does not send us out of fellowship with God. Life's trials do not throw us into panic.

You see, when Christ Jesus is our Savior and we make our heavenly Father the Lord of our lives, nothing can cause us to panic.

Why? Because the answer to everything in life is living on the inside of us in the presence of the Holy Spirit. We have no reason to panic, no matter what the challenge.

You may ask, "How can I experience an unshakable peace?"

# First, recognize your utter dependence upon God.

This truth is the absolute key to experiencing the peace of God, a peace that surpasses all human understanding and protects us against every enemy in life.

# Next, cast your burden upon the Lord in prayer.

> **Be anxious for nothing, but in everything by prayer and supplication, with thanksgiving, let your requests be made known to God." —Philippians 4:6**

# Number three, place your faith in God.

Trust in this God who said, "Cast your burdens upon Me and I will care for you." (Psalm 55:22, paraphrase)

Finally, focus your attention upon God
and not the cause of the anxiety.

focus on God

Psalm 55 beautifully tells of the benefits of trusting God:

**Cast your burden upon the LORD and He will**

**sustain you; He will never allow the righteous**

**to be shaken** —Psalm 55:22 NASB

No matter how heavy the burden seems—regardless of what has caused you anxiety, trial, and heartache—that verse encourages, "Just cast it upon the Lord and He will sustain you. He'll keep you steady. He'll keep you strong. He will never allow the righteous to be shaken."

Psalm 68:19 (NASB), contains a wonderful promise: "Blessed be the Lord, who daily bears our burden . . ."

Now what does the psalmist mean by "daily bears our burden"? Simply, that with the dawning of each new day, God is ready to take the burden of cares from us.

## Let it go

As long as I hold onto the burden and focus on its cares, then I am responsible to carry it. Its full weight is on me, and it may cause many problems.

> But if my total dependence is on the Lord, I have the freedom to release the burden. The promise is that He will daily bear it. We are to cast all our burdens on Him, because He cares for us (1 Peter 5:7). He does not intend for us to live with anxieties and fears. God wants us to have a life filled with joy and peace.

## Prayer is essential

If you pray only at mealtime or just when you get into bed
at night, then you are not living a life of absolute dependence
upon God. When a time of testing comes, if prayer is not a
part of your lifestyle, you're going to have a problem. In
addition, if prayer isn't a part of your lifestyle, then you're
going to have a problem with anxieties. Your life might be like
a roller coaster, up and down, full of anxiety and fear instead
of a continuing peace in God.

It is impossible to experience unshakable peace apart from a
powerful prayer life.

## Amid an anxiety epidemic

Our culture's anxiety level has reached such a height that people shoot and kill others and never give it a thought. We're so full of anxiety and fear and that we can hardly live with each other. How did our national feeling of peace and safety go away?

The reason is clear. Somehow we have decided we are so smart that we don't need God. We have taken Him out of the school, out of the home, out of our government—what do we have left? The result is a society minus the benefits of God's provision.

## We have peace and confidence

The Bible encourages us to trust this God who daily bears our burdens. Trust this God in whom there is a peace beyond human comprehension. Trust this God who promises, "in quietness and confidence shall be your strength" (Isaiah 30:15). Trust this God who made this wonderful statement:

> **"Do not fear, for I am with you; do not anxiously look about you, for I am your God. I will strengthen you, surely I will help you, surely I will uphold you with my righteous right hand."** —Isaiah 41:10 NASB

Put your faith in the God who is living on the inside of you in the person of the Holy Spirit.

Put your faith in the God who longs to bear your burdens.

Focus your attention upon God and not the cause of the anxiety.

What happens when you begin to pray? Your focus turns to God.

My friend, I promise you there is no panic when your faith is in God. Nothing can shake that peace when you and I are living in absolute, utter dependence upon Him. You will experience the buffer of faith and prayer, and when those trials come, you won't lose your peace. The Bible promises, "Thou wilt keep him in perfect peace whose mind is stayed on thee . . . " (Isaiah 26:3, KJV). When my focus is on Him, everything else must be viewed through His truth.

## The Creator can handle it

My friend, the Creator of the universe—all the galaxies, stars, suns, and moons—can handle any and all of the burdens you may experience in life.

> No test or trial surprises Him. He is aware of every circumstance that you might go through. You don't have to live in anxiety; you can live in complete trust and true peace.

> If I could point to one key to peace, it's the principle of focus. Focus on God. Then no matter what challenge comes before you, God's peace is available to you in Christ.

## Prayer for Peace

*Father, how thankful we are for Your love,*
*that You love us enough to care for us when we can't*
*care for ourselves. Sometimes little things that*
*we ought to be able to handle, we can't.*
*But You've made an awesome promise, and all of*
*heaven stands behind it. Grant us the wisdom to live*
*in a peace that passes all human understanding.*
*Keep and guard our hearts in Christ Jesus*
*through every trial in life. We ask this in the*
*name of Jesus and for His sake. Amen.*

# GOD

COMFORTS US

# CHAPTER FOUR

# September 11th, 2001

After the horrible attacks upon the United States, the American people responded in the most awesome fashion. People began recovery in almost every single sector of our society. Yet a dark cloud still seemed to hover because of all the pain and suffering that followed the assault.

When we think of the death toll, the continuing threat of war, and the warnings of possible future attacks, the cloud still hangs over us. This uncertainty has caused us to feel fear, hurt, and pain.

You may ask, "How can we handle this?"

After the September 11, 2001, attack, I began to understand the profound sorrow penetrating my heart. I felt something I'd never felt before. I wanted to cry, but the pain was too deep. I wanted to talk, but I didn't have any words to say that seemed to fit.

The natural response is for us to disconnect. We cannot fix it or change it. We feel like ants facing a mountain. All we can do is stare at the challenge ahead and wonder what to do next. Our hearts cry, "Father! This attack didn't happen somewhere far away. This is our country. These are two of our major cities."

We may ask, "God, what's going on?"

# Comfort is abundant through Christ

Pain is personal. Fear is personal. Sometimes these emotions come to those who never thought they would feel them. Then all of a sudden, there's this cloud hovering. All we have to ask is, "How do we deal with it?"

As Paul wrote his second letter to the Corinthian church, he began by informing his readers of what he had discovered in life amid all of his pain and his suffering:

**Paul, an apostle of Jesus Christ by the will of God, and Timothy our brother, to the church of God which is at Corinth with all the saints who are throughout Achaia: Grace to you and peace from God our Father and the Lord Jesus Christ. Blessed be the God and Father of our Lord Jesus Christ, the Father of mercies and God of all comfort, who comforts us in all our affliction so that we will be able to comfort those who are in any affliction with the comfort with which we ourselves are also comforted by God. For just as the sufferings of Christ are ours in abundance, so also our comfort is abundant through Christ.** —2 Corinthians 1:1-5 NASB

# Our hearts yearn for comfort.

Unfortunately, most people do not know where to find comfort. They've got friends who sometimes pat them on the back and say, "Well, just cheer up." The truth is that sometimes when you're hurting, you don't want somebody to say, "Cheer up!"

You would like to respond, "Look, just don't say that to me. I'm not in the mood to be cheered up. I am hurting and now my pain is so deep I can't even explain it. Telling me to cheer up is not what I need. Don't tell me everything is going to be all right. I am not certain right now that it's going to be all right."

All of us don't suffer the same way; all of us don't feel the same hurt. We don't all feel the same pain, because we don't see it from the same perspective. But it is important that we see it the way God sees it.

# Run to the Rock

There is a place,
there is a way,
there is Someone we can run to in the deepest sorrows of life.

No matter what the reason or the nature of your loss,
no matter how deep your pain may be,
no matter how heavy your heart or uncertain you may
be about the future,

## there is an answer.

You can be absolutely assured that our heavenly Father will
take you through any trial. No matter how deep your pain,
no matter how futile and hopeless you may feel, our heavenly
Father will bring you through it. He is the God of all comfort.
That means whatever you need, He's going to be there to
match that need.

God understands that sometimes people
can hurt so deeply that they cannot hear.

They do not want to talk. They're so overwhelmed with the
shock and the loss that they don't know how to deal with it.
This especially is true of those who do not know Jesus Christ
as their Savior. They don't understand forgiveness. They don't
understand the love of God. They do not understand the
character of almighty God and His unconditional love that
strengthens us in these times.

But God understands every single person. He never gets
upset. He doesn't get angry with us for being angry about
pain. God understands.

We have a God who has provided all the comfort we will ever need to face every single challenge of life.

His comfort is available in an instant.

## Does He instantly heal our pain? Not necessarily.

Before Jesus returned to the Father, He promised to send the Holy Spirit, who will be our Comforter, our helper (John 14:26). That very word, "comforter," in the original language is the word "parakletos," which means "one called alongside." This means that God, our Comforter, desires to involve Himself in our hurt and in our pain. The Holy Spirit comes along side of us to help us and encourage us.

Jesus said the Holy Spirit will be in us, with us and upon us forever. Every single child of God—everyone who has received the Lord Jesus Christ as Savior—has a person of the Trinity living within. That is the person of the Holy Spirit.

Jesus spoke often about comfort.

He says . . .

> **"Come to Me all you who labor and are heavy laden, and I will give you rest."** —Matthew 11:28

He says . . .

> **"Take My yoke upon you and learn from Me"** —Matthew 11:29

He says . . .

> **"I am gentle and lowly in heart"** —Matthew 11:29

and He promises . . .

> **"You will find rest for your souls."** —Matthew 11:29

I will comfort you in those troublesome times.

# Our heavenly Father loves us

He loves us unconditionally. He's a God of all comfort in all our affliction, whether the pain comes from the loss of something or the loss of someone. Whether it's some other type of pain, heartache, or suffering. Whether it is a trial that happens physically to your life. Whether it comes as some form of sickness or even facing death. He is the God of all comfort.

# A present help

When the Bible says He's the God of all comfort, it doesn't make any difference what our affliction is; He's always there, always ready, always sufficient to do it. What's His method? His method is presence. When you and I are going through difficulty and hardship, what do we need above everything else? Somebody to tell us what to do? No. Because oftentimes we're not ready to be told what to do. We need presence. Sometimes it's quiet presence, just being there. Jesus' promise of presence is, "I'm going to send you the Holy Spirit. He'll be in you, with you, and upon you forever." (John 14:16–17 paraphrase)

# Power of the Word

I think about how God uses His Word. There is a very special verse that powerfully deal with this subject. Because you see, one of the ways He wants to help comfort us is for us to meditate upon His Word to be reminded of His promises: the promise of His presence, the promise of His forgiveness, the promise of His provision, the promise of the future.

**This is my comfort in my affliction, that**

**Your word has revived me.** —Psalm 119:50 NASB

We must meditate upon God's Word. Don't wait until tragedy happens; meditate on God's Word now because it's what keeps us anchored. It keeps us connected to thinking the way God does. It keeps us anchored to the promises of God. It keeps us anchored to the truth that we need to live in and live by, the principles that will guide us through the most difficult times of life. We are to meditate upon His Word.

This is my comfort in times of affliction, that God's Word has revived me. When I feel down and don't know which way to turn, then I get into the Word and begin to be revived.

# A great host of comforters

God is continuously our comfort. His comfort is available
in every single circumstance of life. His purpose is not just
to relieve us, because comfort means to relieve someone of
pain or stress. What does God have in mind? That by
successfully dealing with life's difficulties, we become
equipped to comfort other people.

If ever there has been a time when God needs a great host
of comforters, this is the time.

The Spirit of the Lord God is upon Me . . .

He has sent Me to heal the brokenhearted,

to proclaim liberty to the captives. . . —Isaiah 61:1

I wonder how many times have you said to the Lord, "Dear Lord, I want You to use me. I don't want a lot of pain in my life, but I'm willing to be used." Sorry, God does not work that way.

If you want to be used by God, get ready to hurt. If you want to be a comforter, then get ready to suffer. If you want to be someone who can really encourage others, then you must be a person who's walked through the valley of discouragement, surrounded by hurt, suffering, and loss.

God is equipping you and me to be vessels of love, healing, and restoration to a world of people filled with pain, hate, and fear.

# Trials qualify us to be used by God as comforters.

Comforters are equipped to listen quietly and hold a weeping friend. These are people who will never just say, "Don't cry. Cheer up. Everything will be okay."

Listen carefully.

> When somebody's hurting and going through pain, they don't need to hear, "Don't cry." Let them cry. Don't tell them, "Don't feel that way." They have to feel that way, at least for the moment. Don't tell them, "You should, you ought, you must." Those are not the healing words for people who are hurting.

Sometimes no words can help. People just want to be held. They just want to be heard. They just want to be able to cry and feel that it is okay. They want to be able to express their anger and you not be shocked.

**. . . Put my tears into Your bottle . . .** —Psalm 56:8

## Jesus wept

When John recorded the story of Jesus with Mary and Martha after the death of Lazarus, he included this simple, profound detail: "Jesus wept" (John 11:35). What was He crying about? Was He weeping because Lazarus was dead? No. Because Jesus knew He was going to raise Lazarus from the dead.

What made the Son of God sad enough to weep? The answer is compassion.

He was feeling the hurt and the pain that two of His very dearest friends felt. He wept because He felt their loss. He understood their hurt and their pain. He knew that He was going to absolutely shock them when He stood before that tomb and said, "Roll back that stone."

# Empowered by pain

**Who comforts us in all our affliction so that
we will be able to comfort those who are
in any affliction with the comfort with which
we ourselves are comforted by God.**

—2 Corinthians 1:4 NASB

You are able to provide comfort only when you have been
through the fire. Only because you've been in the furnace of
affliction. Only because you've suffered loss. Only because you
know the depth of hurt and pain. Only because you know
what loneliness, emptiness, uncertainty, and fear are all about.
Then you will be ready to comfort others.

# New belief

Our Heavenly Father is ready to comfort everyone who will allow Him. You may say, "Well anybody who is suffering will certainly allow God to comfort them." Not necessarily. Some people push Him away. Some people want no part of Him. And some people are hurt so badly they just withdraw.

Your hurt and pain may become so deep and so intense that you desperately reach for help in new directions that stretch your beliefs. So you pray. You ask for help, healing, forgiveness. Then the Lord Jesus Christ comes into your heart and forgives you of your sin. The Holy Spirit comes to live inside of you. You're able to experience a sense of comfort, peace, and joy even amid the hurt. Deep down inside you know God will bring healing in His perfect timing.

**In this is love, not that we loved God, but that He loved us and sent His Son ...** —1 John 4:10 NASB

## Begin to ask God . . . Lord, show me.

What are You saying to me at this point in my life?
What are You trying to teach me in all this?
How do You want to change my life?

You know what will happen? God not only will relieve you of
the pain and the hurt, you will begin to understand something
about Him that you've never understood. You'll begin to see
Him in a different light. Soon you'll discover an inner joy
because of what is changing in your life. Amid all of your loss,
the Lord Jesus Christ is filling up the emptiness, filling up
the void.

## Though you cannot see Him

and touch Him physically, you know Jesus is so real in your life that the pain and the loneliness is disappearing, little-by-little. Now you have someone you can talk to anytime, anywhere—the Lord Jesus Christ. He said, "Ask and it shall be given you, seek and you shall find, knock and it shall be opened to you" (Matthew 7:7). He is there to hear your plea, there to understand your hurt, and there to put His loving arms around you and hold you in His loving care. He's there, but you must be willing to receive His love.

Jesus puts believers in relationship with one another. He wants us to share life's hurt and pain with each other. You see, each of us needs others.

## Make Me a Comforter

*Father, how grateful we are that You accept us
where we are. You can use every experience in our life.
Some things we would rather have escaped,
but You wouldn't allow it. You were in the process
of sharpening us, pruning, sanding, and sifting us,
equipping us to be strong and effective servants.*

*I pray in Jesus' name that every one who is reading
this would be willing to say to You, "Father,
I'm available to be a comforter to others. Whatever I
need to better understand, send it my way.
Make me an effective vessel in whom You will be
well pleased and through whom someone else will find
You as their Savior so their heart may be healed."
In Jesus' name. Amen.*

# Rejoice in your trials

Peter, an apostle of Jesus Christ, to those who reside
    as aliens, scattered throughout Pontus, Galatia,
    Cappadocia, Asia, and Bithynia, who are chosen
    according to the foreknowledge of God the Father,
    by the sanctifying work of the Spirit, to obey Jesus
    Christ and be sprinkled with His blood; May grace
    and peace be yours in the fullest measure.
    Blessed be the God and Father of our Lord Jesus
    Christ, who according to His great mercy has
    caused us to be born again to a living hope through
    the resurrection of Jesus Christ from the dead, to
    obtain an inheritance which is imperishable and
    undefiled and will not fade away, reserved in heaven
    for you, who are protected by the power of God
    through faith for a salvation ready to be revealed
    in the last time ... you greatly rejoice, even though
    now for a little while, if necessary, you have been

distressed by various trials, that the proof of your faith, being more precious than gold which is perishable, even though tested by fire, may be found to result in praise and glory and honor at the revelation of Jesus Christ; and though you have not seen Him, you love Him, and though you do not see Him now, but believe in Him, you greatly rejoice with joy inexpressible and full of glory, obtaining as the outcome of your faith the salvation of your souls.

—1 Peter 1:1-9 NASB

# How we respond

The key is not how you and I look at trials and heartaches in our lives, but how we respond to them. That is, how do we react when things don't go our way? How do we respond when we're facing opposition, trials, and all kinds of disappointments in life?

Believers must learn how to respond in a fashion that keeps us resting in the Lord, but also that bears witness to God's faithfulness. That is the testimony that unbelievers need to see when they face life's struggles. They should be able to watch us to learn the Source of our strength. The key is having the correct perspective.

In order to keep the right perspective when the bottom is dropping out and we don't know what to do next, we must find our position of security in Him.

We must reaffirm three things:

> We are chosen in Christ Jesus.
> We are born again.
> We are protected by the power of God.

We aren't secure on the basis of our performance, our conduct, or our behavior.

We aren't secure on the basis of how we respond to trials and heartaches.

We are secure in the person of Jesus Christ—on the basis of His sacrificial, all-sufficient, substitutionary death at Calvary. The moment we received Him, having been chosen by Him, a new birth experience took place in our lives, and God assumed the responsibility of protecting us. It isn't a matter of us holding onto Him—because in our weak faith oftentimes we might let go—but He holds onto us. We are protected and secured in Him.

So, when all evil breaks loose and we don't know what to do, one thing is certain—God is holding onto us.

God has assumed the responsibility of protecting us.

## Broken and blessed

It has been necessary down through the ages for the church of the Lord Jesus Christ to undergo persecution in order to grow. It is necessary in your life and my life for God to purify us and to empower us and to equip us to do the work of ministry. Oftentimes, it is very necessary for us to suffer.

You show me a man or woman who has been broken and I'll show you a person who has a great potential to serve God. They will work with greater authority, fruitfulness, and productivity than any person who has managed to avoid stressful trials and tribulations in life.

> None of us likes to see others broken—and we surely don't want to be broken ourselves—but would you not agree that the times in your life when you have grown the strongest have been the times you have suffered the most?

The apostle Peter teaches that in trials you have a right to rejoice (1 Peter 1:6).

He says "greatly rejoice" that is, with great jubilance and assurance, with rejoicing and happiness in your heart.

He says rejoice "even though now for a little while"—that is, for a short season of time in your life, because of necessity, you are going to be under distress. Rejoice because of these manifold trials, these heartaches, these times of temptation and suffering that you're undergoing.

What is the promised outcome of this? Peter points to the reason for joy. We have a right to expect and anticipate that every trial will be profitable.

Peter says "that the proof of your faith," the testing of your faith, is:

> ... much more precious than gold which is perishable, even though tested by fire ... —1 Peter 1:7 NASB

## Perfect faith

God isn't satisfied with a little faith, or even great faith;
He wants perfect faith.

> LITTLE FAITH says "Oh, I know He can. Will
>     He? I know He can."
> GREAT FAITH says, "I know He can and,
>     Hallelujah, I know He will."
> PERFECT FAITH says, "It's as good as done.
>     God made the promise."

God wants us to live in absolute confidence—unwavering,
unswerving confidence—that if He says He's going to do a
thing, we know He's going to do it. It doesn't make any
difference whether or not the world agrees.

# What happens when you face something you can't handle?

You cry out, "Oh, God!" and you fall in prayer on bended knee. You reach out to God. You search your heart, search your life, repent of sin, get things cleaned up so that you know absolutely, without a shadow of a doubt, that you're in a spiritual place where your prayers are being heard and you can hear from God.

You pray, "God, I want to be sure that I am hearing You. I don't want my personal opinion. I'm not being influenced by somebody else. God, this is of You, and I humble myself before You. Search my life, cleanse my life, purify my heart. God, whatever is necessary, do it. I want to be sure to respond correctly to this situation."

> He who dwells in the secret place of the Most High
>
> Shall abide under the shadow of the Almighty.
>
> I will say of the Lord, "He is my refuge and
>
> my fortress; My God, in Him I will trust." . . .
>
> Under His wings you shall take refuge.
>
> —Psalm 91:1-4

Did you know that God gets excited when you and I are obedient to Him? He gives us these big tests, and we plunge through trusting Him. How do we come out on the other side? Stronger in our faith, purer in heart. God wants to bless us. He is ready to bless us. He anticipates the blessing of obedience from His children.

> . . . and though you have not seen Him, you love
>
> Him, and though you do not see Him now, but
>
> believe in Him, you greatly rejoice with joy
>
> inexpressible and full of glory . . . —1 Peter 1:8 NASB

Peter was writing to people who had not seen the Lord Jesus Christ. When you and I go through difficulties and we respond correctly—when God brings us through the valley—not only is our faith proven and found trustworthy, but our personal relationship with Jesus Christ deepens. There's no way to go through heartaches, trials, and tribulations without loving Jesus more. Our faith in Him grows stronger, and we find our contentment and joy in Christ.

The largest single blessing I have received from all of the trials I've encountered is what I've learned about God. It is a truth that I have known all of my life and preached to others. God just keeps reminding me of this fact. I have learned in a deeper way the meaning of these three words:

## God is faithful.

Never-ending, everlasting, reliable. Faithful!

# What is the benefit of knowing about God's faithfulness?

You love Him more. You believe Him more. You are more and more satisfied with Him.

> The more you love Jesus Christ, the less you love this world. Why? Because you don't need it. The more you fall in love with Him, the less you need everything else in life. Material things don't have a dominant, all-consuming place in your heart. So, when you understand the truth, trials aren't so bad after all. What's the end result? Your faith is going to be proven and stronger. It is going to be purified. That makes it more powerful. It is going to have the praise-worthiness of Jesus Christ. Your love for Jesus is going to be greater. Your belief in Him is going to be stronger, and your joy and contentment and happiness with Him are going to make you contented in life with the Lord Jesus Christ.

I've never met a cozy Christian
who God actually used.

Some say, "Don't bother me. I like it cozy, convenient, and
easy. Just don't mess with me." Or "I'm willing to come to
church, but just don't ask me to get involved with the difficult
things. I am not interested in serving and getting involved in
other people's lives."

Well, if you want to go to heaven that way, you can. But when
you get there, you are going to be extremely disappointed.
There are rewards for the believer. You cannot sit on the
sidelines watching life pass by and expect to hear God say,
"Well, done, good and faithful servant."

What is God doing? God has us in school here on earth.
I don't know about you, but I want to make an "A". I want
to be on His dean's list when it comes to responding properly
because I know what happens next: Everything in us of
any value whatsoever becomes more and more useful and
valuable to God. This does not mean that God loves us
more—He can't love us any more than He already, perfectly
does—but we can become more valuable to Him.

God is excited when we obey Him and when we're growing
in Him.

## Fulfill Your Will in Us

*Father, we thank You for loving us.*
*We wouldn't have it any other way than the way*
*You've made it. We don't want convenience*
*and comfort and coziness. We want character.*
*We want Christ-likeness. We want You, Lord Jesus,*
*to fulfill Your great purpose for our lives.*
*This is our prayer in Jesus' name. Amen.*

GOD

IS IN CONTROL

In Him we have redemption through His blood, the forgiveness of sins, according to the riches of His grace which He made to abound toward us in all wisdom and prudence, having made known to us the mystery of His will, according to His good pleasure which He purposed in Himself, that in the dispensation of the fullness of the times He might gather together in one all things in Christ—both which are in heaven and which are on earth— in Him. In Him also we have obtained an inheritance, being predestined according to the purpose of Him who works all things according to the counsel of His will . . .

—Ephesians 1:7-11

Is God in charge or is He not?

He is in absolute control.

## King of Kings, Lord of Lords

The Lord Jesus is the key figure of the Book of the Revelation. It is Jesus who stands paramount and supreme above all others. In the fourth and fifth chapters we see Him sitting upon His throne. We find Him in the nineteenth chapter, coming, ruling and reigning. King of Kings, Lord of Lords. If He's the Lord of Lords, that means His power is supreme above all other power.

There's no other power to equal the supreme authority, the absolute, unquestionable control of the sovereign God of this universe. Jesus Christ is His Son.

## God is involved in our lives

We have this assurance: Our heavenly Father—who is in absolute control of all things—is continually involved in our lives every single day. Why? Because He's protecting us, watching over us, and caring for us. To do this He must be involved every day.

He is the sovereign God who has all power and all knowledge. He knows exactly what we need today. He knows exactly how to guide us. He knows how to provide for us. He knows how to protect us.

I love this verse:

> **He rules by His might forever; His eyes keep watch on the nations . . .** Psalm 66:7 NASB

Nobody—dictator, tyrant, you name it—can do anything that has not already been seen by God. Everything and everybody is in His eyesight, in His knowledge, in His grasp, in His power, in His presence, and under His control. Every single person, every single event in life, God knows about it, has control over it. He allows things that are sometimes difficult for us to understand, but He certainly is in control. He makes nations great and also destroys them. He enlarges nations, then He leads them away. He is in absolute control of all of these things.

## Consider the life of David.

David didn't have a Bible. I don't think David had a bunch of scrolls that he would carry around with him. David learned some awesome truths about God by making mistakes. He learned them by failing. He learned them by being faithful. He learned them in fear, he learned them in courage. David gives us a beautiful and comprehensive view of what life is all about. We learn to understand God's response to us and how we ought to respond to Him.

Listen to what David says:

> So David blessed the Lᴏʀᴅ in the sight of all the
> assembly; and David said, "Blessed art Thou,
> O Lᴏʀᴅ God of Israel our father, forever and ever.
> Thine, O Lᴏʀᴅ, is the greatness and the power
> and the glory and the victory and the majesty,
> indeed everything that is in the heavens and
> on the earth; Thine is the dominion, O Lᴏʀᴅ,
> and Thou dost exalt Thyself as head over all.
> Both riches and honor come from Thee, and Thou
> dost rule over all, and in Thy hand is power and
> might; and in it lies in Thy hand to make great,
> and to strengthen everyone. Now therefore, our
> God, we thank Thee, and praise Thy glorious name.
>
> —1 Chronicles 29:10-13 ᴋᴊᴠ

# The king and his sovereign God

Did David believe in the sovereignty of God? Absolutely! You know why he believed? Because all of David's life, God proved it to him.

In the most difficult and trying time—when David was running for his life from Saul—God spared him. When he was in the depths of sin with Bathsheba, God spared him. When his son rebelled against him and tried to take the kingdom, God rescued him, saved him, and kept him as the king. He walked through the fires, rivers, and storms of life. Here's what he discovered: The sovereign God of this universe was guiding, guarding, and providing for him every single step of the way. This God whom you and I serve is the God of this universe, supreme in His power, immeasurable in His love, awesome in His control.

There is nothing outside the absolute total control of almighty God.

> **The angel of the Lord encamps all around about those who fear Him." —Psalm 34:7**

God is our protector. Now, if He chooses for some reason to open the door to something that's painful, are things out of control? No. That door couldn't open unless almighty God allowed it. Remember Romans 8:28. If He allowed it, God intends to turn that pain, hurt, loss, or difficulty into something good in your life.

## Look to the future with confidence.

The future may look a little foggy. It may look a little troublesome. You might have said, "God, I can't see anything good coming."

Here's what I've discovered. After God has promised something, it doesn't make any difference what I feel or what I see, because God promised to make "all things work together for good" (Romans 8:28). I trust with my life that He will do what He said.

> **But He knows the way that I take; when He has tested me, I shall come forth as gold. —Job 23:10**

Here's our problem: We try to help God out.

He most likely ignores our suggestions, to think about it in human terms, because He's already got a plan fully worked out.

> And we have known and believed the love that God has for us. God is love; and he who abides in love abides in God, and God in him. Love has been perfected among us in this: that we may have boldness in the day of judgment; because as He is, so are we in this world. There is no fear in love; but perfect love casts out fear ... —1 John 4:16-18

# What grieves the heart of God . . .

is when we reject His plan that is so absolutely perfect. That
is when we get in trouble! We think that somehow we have
a better plan than does an omniscient God. We think we can
carry out our plan instead of relying on His omnipotence.

How foolish to act apart from the will of God! We must believe
Him no matter what. Why? Because He's the sovereign God
of this universe. He has every single thing under control.
He's looking out for your good and mine. He's going to turn
all these trying circumstances into something good.

# Why worry?

I've had enough years of trials, heartaches, burdens, successes, and failures in life that I can look back and see the fingerprint of the awesome love of God. No matter what I've been through, I see everything as from the hand of God.

Through all of these years, I finally concluded: If He's in control, why am I going to worry? If I really believe that He's in absolute control and He loves me unconditionally, and always chooses the best for me, and is engineering the circumstances of my life, . . . what am I going to worry about?

God has a perfect design for all of our lives.

Well, suppose I made a big mess of my life? Let me remind you of something. God can handle the mess. He can put the most destroyed, broken pieces back together. He knows how to do that.

There are no challenges for God. There is no furrow on His brow and no wringing of His hands. He's a sovereign God. I can get on my knees before Him and tell Him what I think, how I feel, my hurts, my desires, my needs. I don't have to wonder, "Can He do it?" I know this: Because He's a loving Father, He's going to answer my prayer.

For I am persuaded, that neither death, nor life,

nor angels, nor principalities, nor powers,

nor things present, nor things to come, Nor

height, nor depth, nor any other creature,

shall be able to separate us from the love of

God, which is in Christ Jesus our Lord.

—Romans 8:38-39 KJV


...Eye hath not seen, nor ear heard, neither have

entered into the heart of man, the things which

God hath prepared for them that love Him.

—1 Corinthians 2:9 KJV

You may be going through some difficulty and heartache and you've said:

"My pain!" God's in control.
"My hurt!" God's in control.
"But what about this?" God's in control.
"What about my finances?" God's in control.

I understand those struggles. You know what you need to do? You just need to say, "God, I don't understand it all, but I'm going to accept by faith that You're in control. I'm going to watch You straighten out my life."

I think God would reply, "I've been waiting for you to say that for a very long time."

Because He is a master at putting the pieces back together.

# We Pray for Your Reign

*Father, we love You and praise You and bless*

*Your name. We ask that Your Holy Spirit*

*would seal this message tight in our heart.*

*Let it run through our heart, soul,*

*and spirit until we are absolutely consumed*

*with the truth . . . until our God,*

*whose Son is Jesus Christ,*

*is sovereign master controller*

*and the absolute ruler over every aspect*

*of our life. In Jesus' name, amen.*

# Conclusion

Perhaps you have just received some devastating news. You wish you could change what you have heard, but you can't. Your mind fights to accept what you know is true, but your emotions hold you back. All that is within you cries out for hope and understanding. You search for an answer to the question that consumes your mind: "Will everything be all right?"

When we face overwhelming situations, the one thing that brings assurance and hope is the fact that God is in control. No matter what we experience or feel, we can know that He loves us and is working to bring good out of each heartache, difficulty, or disappointment. This one fact has encouraged and strengthened countless hearts. No matter where you turn in the Bible, you will never find a moment when God was out of control or out of touch with His creation. He is our very present help. (Psalm 46:1)

The tragedy is that millions of people around the world remain hopeless and helpless—daily they face heartache, oppression, and trials alone, unaware that God's power and love are available to them. At In Touch Ministries, it is our goal to take the Gospel of Jesus Christ worldwide to as many people as possible, as clearly as possible, as irresistibly as possible, and as quickly as possible, in the power of the Holy Spirit and to the glory of God.

Currently, IN TOUCH is broadcast in 30 languages, accessible in every country around the globe and understandable by half of the world's population. But half is not enough. The Bible tells us that in heaven, there will be believers from every tribe and tongue and people and nation (Revelation 5:9). Therefore, we recognize that our responsibility is to reach the entire world with the Gospel. Toward that end, we have made it our objective to translate the message of Jesus Christ into 100 languages by the year 2012. When we do, more than 92 percent of the world's population will be able to hear it in a language they comprehend. You can be a part of this effort to bring light and hope to a world that is desperate for it. To find out how, call In Touch Ministries at 888-558-3463 or find us on the web at www.itmupdate.org.

Now unto him that is able to keep you from

falling, and to present you faultless before

the presence of his glory with exceeding joy,

To the only wise God our Savior, be glory

and majesty, dominion and power, both now

and ever. Amen. —Jude 1:24,25, KJV

## About the Art

Dr. Charles Stanley has said that if he weren't a pastor, he'd be a nature photographer. His passion for this art has taken him all over the world.

This book features not only Dr. Stanley's words assuring us that God is in control, but also photographs that show us the Creator as seen through the author's camera. Most of these stunning landscapes were captured by Dr. Stanley during his trips in the British Isles, the North American West—especially the Canadian Rockies, the canyons of Utah, and the Tetons of Wyoming—and the South Island of New Zealand.

Dr. Stanley's western North American landscapes appear on the following pages: Cover, 5, 10, 14, 21, 23, 24, 37, 41, 42, 45, 47, 48, 51, 53, 55, 58, 61, 63, 67, 75, 76, 78, 95, 96, 99, 115, 116, 117, 121, 124

Dr. Stanley's New Zealand landscapes appear on the following pages: 8, 13, 18, 26, 30, 31, 38, 57, 73, 82, 105, 107, 109

Dr. Stanley's British Isles landscapes appear on the following pages: 32, 34, 35, 46, 56, 85